aggressive girls, clueless boys

CONVERSATIONS
YOU *MUST* HAVE WITH YOUR SON

[7 QUESTIONS YOU SHOULD ASK YOUR DAUGHTER]

aggressive girls, clueless boys

CONVENANTS

⑦

CONVERSATIONS

YOU *MUST* HAVE WITH YOUR SON

[7 QUESTIONS YOU SHOULD ASK YOUR DAUGHTER]

dennis rainey

with david boehi

FAMILYLIFE®

Little Rock, Arkansas

AGGRESSIVE GIRLS, CLUELESS BOYS:
7 CONVERSATIONS YOU MUST HAVE WITH YOUR SON

FamilyLife Publishing®
5800 Ranch Drive
Little Rock, Arkansas 72223
1-800-FL-TODAY · FamilyLife.com
FLTI, d/b/a FamilyLife®, is a ministry of Campus Crusade for Christ International®

Unless otherwise noted, Scripture quotations are from the Holy Bible, English Standard Version, copyright © 2001 by Crossway Bibles, a division of Good News Publishers. Used by permission. All rights reserved.

Scripture quotations marked (MSG) are taken from *The Message*. Copyright © by Eugene H. Peterson 1993, 1994, 1995, 1996, 2000, 2001, 2002. Used by permission of NavPress Publishing Group.

Scripture quotations marked (NASB) are taken from the New American Standard Bible®. Copyright © 1960, 1962, 1963, 1968, 1971, 1972, 1973, 1975, 1977, 1995 by The Lockman Foundation. Used by permission. (www.Lockman.org)

Names and details in some anecdotes and stories have been changed to protect the identities of the persons involved.

ISBN: 978-1-60200-523-5

Design: Thinkpen Design, Inc., www.thinkpendesign.com

Printed in the United States of America

16 15 14 13 12   1 2 3 4 5

FAMILYLIFE®
Help for today. Hope for tomorrow.

To

"Cookie"

My Bride, Friend, and Soul Mate

Since
September 2, 1972

Thank you for being the right kind of woman
And for not being an *aggressive girl*
When we dated over 40 years ago.
I love doing life with you.

I love you!!!

(I have a surprise for you on our 40th,
but you'll have to close your eyes and hold out
your hands on our anniversary this year to get it.)

Contents

Acknowledgments

FamilyLife, the organization that I serve in, is made up of about 400 of the finest men and women in the world. This book is a reflection of a truly great team that knows how to execute with excellence. Let me apologize in advance for the teammates I may not mention here . . . it's always dangerous to start a list like this, but here goes.

My appreciation and gratefulness go to:

Steve and Pam Thorne for your e-mail and call that basically said my book *Interviewing Your Daughter's Date* was fine and dandy for those parents who had girls, but that you needed help in protecting your sons. Well, here it is. I'm efficient no matter how long it takes!

Bill Eyster for running the ship. Bob Lepine for pushing on the idea of this book. Dave Boehi for going through all those broadcasts and creating the manuscript. Tim Grissom for being a great editor and comrade. Leslie Barner for caring about an elusive cover, title, and layout. Michele English for . . . we both know all that you do. Well, maybe I don't know, so thanks. A host of others whose contributions made this all happen: Steve

Crowell, Rob Tittle, Marc Vail, and Tammy Meyers. A hearty thanks to Michael and Hayley DiMarco, a couple of kindred spirit warriors, on behalf of the next generation, who helped sharpen this sword. Todd Nagel, who didn't do anything to help with this book, but who needs ongoing forgiveness for being a Longhorn.

And the love of my life since 1972, Barbara.

1

How Could This Happen?

It was just a routine check. When Susan and Tom gave thirteen-year-old Josh his first cell phone, they told him that they would occasionally look through his text messages. But Susan was completely unprepared for what she found that Saturday morning.[1]

She waded through a couple hundred short, inane messages, more than slightly confused by the shorthand that kids use when texting. She was struck by the fact that Josh and his friends seemed to text each other more than they actually talked. And then something different popped up. There was no confusion about this message:

If you could have sex with me, would you?

---

[1] To protect anonymity, I have changed the names and some details in the stories I will share in this book.

> **We've raised him in a good home. How could this happen?**

Her mind spinning in disbelief, Susan continued looking through the texts. And a story began to emerge: While hanging out with some friends a couple weeks earlier, Josh had met a girl from another school. They began texting each other the next day, and it was clear that she had quickly begun pursuing him sexually. With suggestive language, she talked about what she wanted to do with him, and within a few days she lured him into sneaking out of his house in the middle of the night so they could meet for sex at a relative's empty apartment. "I'm wearing a thong," she wrote. "Can you sneak out tonight?"

Susan was so stunned that she could hardly breathe. *Josh has never had a girlfriend, never even kissed a girl,* she thought. *We've raised him in a good home. How could this happen?*

In a daze, she found her husband and filled him in. He was just as shocked. They knew they would someday need to talk with Josh's younger sisters about how to handle boys who wanted sex, but they never expected this.

A shift in our culture

Sex among teenagers is old news, unfortunately, as is aggressive boys pursuing girls, men pursuing women, and adult women pursuing adult men. But a growing number of parents like Tom and Susan are learning that something has shifted in our culture over the last couple of decades. Increasingly, girls are aggressively pursuing boys—in high school, middle school, and even earlier—in numbers we never saw in the past. The rules have changed, and many parents are asking for help in how to protect their young sons. This shift has caught them by surprise, and they don't know what to do.

A few years ago, I wrote a book entitled *Interviewing Your Daughter's Date*. I challenged dads to man up and take steps to protect the purity of their daughters. Interviewing a young man who wants to date your daughter is a good way to filter out the undesirables, so to speak, and call young men to treat a young lady's sexuality with respect and nobility.

After that book was published, I heard stories about fathers who stepped up and had some great heart-to-heart conversations with young men. But what I didn't expect were the messages from readers and *FamilyLifeToday*® radio listeners asking for help in protecting their sons from aggressive girls. Here is a sample:

> We have three grown daughters and a sixteen-year-old son. You would think our family would have experienced plenty of aggressive behavior from boys toward

our daughters, but nothing compares with what I see our son going through.

I have a fourteen-year-old son. He is contacted by girls all the time on Facebook and texts. One went so far as to take pictures of herself in scant clothing (in my opinion) and send them to him. This occurred without the knowledge of her parents and when my son was in seventh grade.

My ten-year-old son was enticed by another fifth grade girl via e-mail to open another e-mail account so that I couldn't monitor it. But I found it and canceled it. She is sending e-mail messages and e-cards to him and two of his friends in a love quadrangle that she's brilliantly orchestrated.

I have two sons who attend public school. Recently, they were talking at the dinner table about the girls that grab their butts in the hallways. My husband and I were shocked. They said, "Welcome to public school, Mom!"

I have a thirteen-year-old boy, an eleven-year-old boy, and a seven-year-old boy. All of them have been pursued by girls. I think what shocks me the most is the encouragement from the parents of the girls who mistakenly think it is "cute."

We recently were hunting for a church nearer to our home. We found a good one, except that girls in the youth group zeroed in to our son like heat-seeking missiles.

Our son is thirteen, fun loving, friendly, and extremely handsome, or "hot" as many young females have expressed to him. He's been asked to "go out" by high school girls and girls his own age, too. He talks to us about stuff we never even thought he'd be dealing with at his Christian school. Girls will walk right up to him, even at the grocery store while shopping with me . . . his mom! He needs to know how to deal with girls who ask brazen questions, wanting his approval and affection.

The problem with aggressive behavior, especially when sexual in nature, is that its appetite is never satisfied. Each generation finds new and more adventuresome ways of expressing their urges. On a recent flight, I was seated next to the principal of a Christian high school. As we swapped stories, I told him that I was working on a book about the increasing sexual aggressiveness of girls in our culture. He locked on to the message immediately and told me of yet another disturbing trend—a combination of sexual aggression and cyber-bullying. He shared how girls are texting boys, often in the middle of the night, and pushing them to "grind" with them (imitating sex with their clothes on) or pay the price of ridicule and rumor.

"Bad" girls?

There have always been girls who are flirty and crazy about boys, even some girls who could be labeled as "bad girls." You probably remember a few from your own days as a teenager. But now, the "bad girl" problem is becoming more commonplace. Over and over, parents are expressing the same concern: Girls are pursuing their sons more openly and relentlessly than ever before. They are calling, texting, sending suggestive photos, setting up romantic liaisons . . . and they're doing these things at a younger age.

I want to make it very clear that I am not placing all the blame for teenage promiscuity on girls. I also understand that parents need to protect their daughters from aggressive boys, especially as those boys move into the latter years of high school and beyond. A shocking number of men and boys have, and continue to be, sexual predators. I make absolutely no excuses for them. But I am writing this particular book to help those parents who have realized that we also have a growing problem with aggressive girls.

The need for a plan

The fact is that many parents just don't realize how little training they are giving their adolescent and pre-adolescent sons in how to relate to the opposite sex. I'm not just talking about sex education; our boys need to learn what to expect in adolescence—and beyond—and how to handle it. Temptation, lust, and sexual attraction are bearing down on them. They need to be prepared.

> **Temptation, lust, and sexual attraction are bearing down on them. *You* need to prepare them.**

You need to prepare them.

In these pages you will receive time-tested counsel to empower you to teach and equip your son to understand a biblical perspective of sex and how to protect himself from seductive girls who would do him harm. In the coming chapters, you are going to be equipped with:

- An explanation of why girls are preying on your son, so you can understand the problem more clearly. You can work with him to emerge into manhood with integrity.

- Three commitments you need to make as a parent that will keep you engaged in your son's life as he moves through the years of high hormonal temptation.

- Seven conversations you must have with your son. Six of these are founded on passages from the Book of Proverbs and focus on helping your son understand what God says in the Bible about maintaining sexual purity. These conversations are intensely practical and will help you establish boundaries for your son and also prepare him for specific situations he will face with aggressive girls both now and later in adulthood. Each of these chapters ends with a suggested step-by-step guide for directing the conversation with your son.

- Seven questions that you should ask your daughter . . . seven topics that may result in longer discussions with her that will help her understand the sexual power of a woman and how that power needs to be restrained until marriage.

They thought they had more time

Tom and Susan, the parents in the story at the beginning of this chapter, found themselves dropped in the middle of a minefield. Their son, Josh, had never even been on a date, so they were shocked to find that he had become sexually active. When they met with Josh and told him that they knew what was going on, he tried to deny the extent of his involvement. But the evidence was clear, and he finally admitted what he had done.

Tom and Susan immediately took away Josh's cell phone, shut down his Facebook page, and grounded him from going out with friends for a period of time. They made sure he kept busy with school and sports, so that he wouldn't have idle time. And they moved him out of his downstairs bedroom into a room upstairs with his little brother.

The wounds were still fresh when Susan related the story. "Josh knows this isn't what God wants for him." But the future seems unclear. How do you restore a child to a path of purity after he's already lost his virginity . . . at age thirteen? They are praying that God will use the experience for good in Josh's life.

"I wish we had known these things were going on," Susan said. "I think we would have been more prepared."

2

Your Son Is Mostly Clueless.
How About You?

Think of the hormonal revolution that is taking place in a boy as he approaches adolescence. One parent described it as though there had been "an alien takeover of my son's body and life!"

A boy's body is starting to change, and he barely understands it. He starts feeling attracted to girls, and his mind is clouded by a potent, combustible mixture of fear, anger, confusion, curiosity, and sexual energy.

He and his friends are starting to talk and joke about sex. They are frequently exposed to sexual images and dialogue in the media, but they really don't understand what to make of it all. Many boys will look at pornography on the Internet, and while they are fascinated and stimulated, they are also nervous and perhaps a little ashamed.

He thinks about sex almost constantly. He really, really wants to "do it"! He will likely start masturbating.

He's probably murky about what it means to be a man. Does it mean acting tough? Having sex? Being the first one in his herd to take a girl to bed?

All this swirls in his head. He doesn't understand sex and certainly not romance. In short, he is *really* confused. Clueless. The alien takeover has begun.

> I know that if girls had solicited me when I was in my pre-teen and teen years, there is no way I could have said no. I just don't know how the average boy is even able to say no.

Want to make it worse? Let a girl start pursuing him. She may be someone in his class, or she may be someone older. She tells him he's cute, he's hot, and she'd really like to hang out with him. She leaves notes in his locker and backpack. She calls him and texts him seemingly non-stop. If he is under twelve, he may not like this attention. But the older he is, the more he will be flattered. If the girl is older, he thinks, *I must really be THE MAN for her to pay attention to me.*

Then her texts become more suggestive, and she starts sending him racy photos. Now his hormones shift into overdrive. And then one day at school she whispers to him, "I want to hook up." Here's his chance to do what he has been dreaming about.

What are the chances that this boy has the character, maturity, and wisdom to handle a situation like this?

Why is this happening?

One father told me, "I know that if girls had solicited me when I was in my pre-teen and teen years, there is no way I could have said no. I just don't know how the average boy is even able to say no."

Many of the parents who have written me have been surprised at the increasingly aggressive attitude they have seen in the girls who have pursued their sons. But think about some of the ways our culture has changed in the years since you were a teenager.

1. *A growing number of children are growing up without the positive influence of an intact marriage.* With our high rate of divorce and out-of-wedlock births, we have a generation of sons and daughters who hardly know their fathers or who are forced to split their time between mom's house and dad's. The only time they see their parents interact is when they are arguing over money, visitation schedules, or their new girlfriend or boyfriend. These children never

see a healthy model of a male-female relationship. Many boys are not shown or taught what it means to be a man. And without even realizing it, girls seek to fill their need for male love, attention, and affirmation by preying upon these unsuspecting and curious boys.

2. *Popular media relentlessly questions gender and sexual roles and promotes teenage sexuality.* Many of us see so many sexual references and images that we are becoming numb to them; we barely even notice. Yet this culture shapes the attitudes and beliefs of our children much more than we care to admit. Culturally, they are told it's cool to experiment sexually, as long as they practice safe sex. Traditional male-female relationships are hopelessly old-fashioned. And if you doubt me, take a look at the television shows, movies, magazines, and websites that are popular with teens. I think you'll be surprised, and I hope you'll be disturbed at what the media is teaching our children.

3. *Much more than in the past, girls are exhorted to be aggressive in all areas of their lives.* It is one thing to encourage girls to excel and pursue their dreams. The problem is encouraging a *lifestyle of aggression*—doing whatever it takes to get what they want, no matter who they hurt—especially using their sexuality to exert power over men.

4. *Many parents pull away too quickly from their children.* Parenting feels much easier when your children are in the relatively easy years of ages five through eleven. This is a time when they want to spend time with you, they listen to you, they think you are wise. But as those same children enter adolescence, they begin acting more independently. They want to spend more time with their friends than with you. They argue with you more frequently and question your wisdom . . . and sanity. Some of this is normal. Children *need* to become independent and to grow up. And that means that their relationship with their parents will change. But you cannot—you must not—pull away from them. Not now, not yet. Not in one of the most vulnerable seasons they will face.

I remember a conversation with a fifteen-year-old girl. I asked her, "How would you feel about your dad interviewing your dates?"

"Oh, I don't know about that," she replied. Then she thought some more. "Well, it depends on what areas he'd talk to my dates about. And what areas would be off limits."

I said, "Well, what if nothing was off limits?"

She said, "Well, I wouldn't want him talking about physical boundaries. Now, emotional boundaries, that's okay. If we could have a conversation about emotional boundaries, I could see how a fifteen-year-old needs her dad to protect her there. But I'm not ready for my dad to protect the sexual boundary."

That's a good snapshot of how adolescents think. They don't know what they don't know. It shows how critical it is for a parent to stay engaged during these years, because your kids need you now, more than ever. Without your involvement, they will "go with the flow" and enlist in "Teen Boot Camp," where they will get their training and advice on critical areas like this from their peers and the media.

Passive and confused versus aggressive and daring

The youth culture is filled with girls who are more assertive than ever in relationships. It is important to note that, while some of those who pursue your sons may have evil intent, others are simply young girls who don't know any better. Because they are imitating the culture, they are just doing what they think they are supposed to do.

At the same time, boys are becoming more passive in relationships and more confused about their sexuality. As a *New York Times* writer put it, "After a half-century during which generations of young women were advised to never even call a boy on the telephone, it is now teenage girls who not only do the calling, but who often initiate romantic and even sexual activity. Whether they are influenced by the trickle-down effects of feminism, which has taught girls to be assertive in all areas of life, or have internalized the images of sexually powerful women in popular culture, American girls are more daring than ever."[1]

In a world where all the old rules have been thrown out, it is critical for us to pass on to our children a biblical model for relationships. A man and woman in a biblical marriage have a way of relating where the man loves, leads, and serves his wife, giving up his life for her. In turn, she supports him, believes in him, respects him and, encourages him as he attempts to lead. When that happens, you have children who can begin to feel secure about who they are as a boy or girl, growing into adults. But when it doesn't happen and girls are the aggressors and boys are rewarded for being passive, our sons and daughters grow up confused about what it means to be a man or woman.

> **In a world where all the old rules have been thrown out, it is critical for us to pass on to our children a biblical model for relationships.**

As your son moves into the teen years, he is not a grown man yet. He may think he is, and at times he may even surprise you by acting in pleasingly mature ways. But he is still mostly clueless, especially about the lure of sex. He needs you to coach him and train him and equip him for life. The lessons you pass on will most certainly be used to guide him for the rest of his adult life.

3

Three Radical Convictions

When Patricia's seventh-grade son, Blake, and his best friend asked if they could go to the hot tub in their apartment complex, she thought it was a strange request. "Are you meeting anyone there?" she asked. They said they weren't, and she agreed to let them go.

But then she began thinking . . .

Earlier that evening Blake had asked if his new girlfriend, Lindsey, could eat dinner with them. Patricia said that it wasn't a good night and then learned that Lindsey and her mother were on her doorstep at that very moment! Lindsey had told her mother that she was invited to dinner with Blake's family. But Patricia held her ground and told Lindsey, "Maybe another night."

Patricia was uneasy about this relationship. Blake and Lindsey had met at school and then began exchanging text messages. But it was clear that Lindsey was directing the relationship and was trying to manipulate events to spend time with Blake.

Now she wondered who had come up with the idea of using the hot tub.

Over the next half hour, Patricia snuck over to the hot tub several times to see if Blake and his friend were alone. Something told her to keep checking, and on her fifth reconnaissance mission, she discovered that Lindsey had joined them. Furious, she ordered the boys to return to the apartment, and she told Lindsey to go home.

But the story didn't end there. Lindsey's mother called a while later in a panic. She had gone on a date with her boyfriend, leaving Lindsey alone, and had returned to find an empty apartment. Patricia was stunned; she thought Lindsey had gone to the hot tub with her mother's approval. Now she felt guilty for ordering Lindsey to return home.

Fortunately Lindsey got home okay; Patricia later learned she had walked three miles in the dark between apartment complexes. Patricia had a long conversation with the boys that night. Blake had been flattered by Lindsey's attention and eager to see what might happen with his first girlfriend. He certainly wasn't blameless; he went along with Lindsey's plan and perhaps even encouraged her interest. But on another level he was naive about where the relationship was heading and about the ramifications of his deception. Patricia told Blake that it was time to break things off with Lindsey.

As Patricia looked back a few years later, she realized it had been a "perfect opportunity for me to tell Blake about how he should act with girls and what type of situations to avoid. It gave me an opportunity and some credibility to give him the facts and lay it all on the line. He trusts me now and believes that I have his best interests at heart. That's a good thing."

Get involved and stay involved

Patricia was a wise mom, and she did many things right that night. She sensed something wasn't right about the situation, that her son was not telling her the truth. She made a special effort to learn the truth, and when she did she nipped the problem before it got worse.

One thing impresses me more than anything else: *she acted*. She checked and rechecked. She didn't retreat. She got involved and stayed involved.

It takes a lot of courage for dads and moms to step up and guide their sons in this sexually permissive and promotional culture.

Our boys are making choices and negotiating relationship challenges earlier than we thought they would, and they need us to be on their team. They may not give the impression that they need—or want—their parents' involvement, but they *really* do. So, as you prepare to step into your son's life, it's important for you to make a few commitments as parents.

The first is, *decide what type of man you want your son to become*.

The biblical call to a young man is to become a noble man, a courageous man, and a spiritual man. If that's what you want for your son, then he needs to learn what God expects of him. He needs to be equipped in how to handle temptation and lust, because this will be one of the earliest tests of his character and faith. And the pattern he sets as an adolescent will influence how he deals with temptation and lust for his entire life.

The next commitment you need to make is, *take responsibility for your son's moral and spiritual training*.

Many parents make the mistake of abdicating this responsibility, relinquishing it to their church, a youth leader, or a Christian school. But getting a child involved with a church youth group does not ensure that he will learn how to make wise choices any more than sending him to a Christian school will insulate him from temptations. Those teenagers in the youth group and school have the same urges and struggles. Assuming they will always exert "good" peer pressure on your son is dangerous. Some of them will encourage him in the wrong direction.

Instead, every parent must come to a firm conviction and say, "*I will be responsible to provide the spiritual and moral instruction for my children. I will not delegate the formation of his character to others. If I don't own it, it's not going to happen.*"

Many parents make the mistake of abdicating this responsibility, relinquishing it to their church, a youth leader, or a Christian school.

Going deeper

If you want your son to grow up to be a man who follows Jesus Christ and if you are willing to provide his spiritual and moral instruction, then a third commitment is necessary: *get involved, and stay involved in your son's life.*

I'm not talking only about involvement in his sporting events, science fair projects, or school dances. I'm talking about going deeper. Learn what's going on in his head and heart. Find activities that you both enjoy and that provide the opportunity to talk and really find out what's happening in his life. Come alongside him to listen when he's ready to talk. Stay involved by teaching, loving, encouraging, exhorting, and seeking to understand.

If he's like most adolescent boys, at some point your son will try to push you out. If he talks at all, he will speak in grunts, mumbles, and shoulder shrugs. Even when he's struggling, he will likely do it in silence. He will act as if he's been cursed with parents who are on "stupid pills."

You will need to push past these barriers and figure out how you can engage him. Because even though he may not admit it, your son actually *wants* you to stay involved. Too many parents pull away from their adolescent sons out of frustration at the very time they need to press in.

> **Even though he may not admit it, your son actually *wants* you to stay involved.**

A son needs a dad who can teach him what it means to be a man and who will model how a man truly surrenders his life to Jesus Christ—a dad who is not passive, but one who initiates leadership and servanthood for his wife and family; a dad who courageously engages his son in conversations and presses into the tough issues (such as pornography) that prey upon a young man's life.

A son also needs a mom who will model the character, modesty, and virtue of a godly woman. She is the very best person to help him understand how girls think and behave. Oftentimes, it is a mom's intuition that can help her son avoid unhealthy relationships with girls whose motives are less than honorable.

And he needs parents who are in agreement about how they are going to help him become the right kind of man who finds the right kind of girl.

Initiating conversations

Think of it: You can prepare your son for what he will experience during his teenage years because you have both lived through adolescence yourselves. You have plenty of stories to tell. Sure, the times are different, but the temptations are still the same.

I know of one father, Chris, who took each of his sons, at age fifteen, on a weekend trip to see a football game at his college alma mater. When they left on the five-hour drive, Chris said, "While I have you in the car, I want to tell you a few stories I've never told you before about some of the things I experienced when I was in college."

He started by telling about an extraordinary experience during his freshman year. He talked about what led him to become a Christian as a sophomore. Without giving the sordid details, he described an impure relationship with a girlfriend during his junior year. He shared how he came to a key point in his life when he needed to decide which path to follow. He chose to break up with the young woman so he could follow Christ with his whole heart.

For Chris, it was a perfect opportunity to talk to his sons—to let them know he was once young and faced the same choices and temptations they experienced. Stories have a way of sticking with a person, and Chris feels those weekends with his sons were key to helping them make responsible choices as they grew older.

This reminds me of the Book of Proverbs, which is basically a collection of wise words passed on from a father to a son. Read Proverbs 4:10–15:

> Hear, my son, and accept my words, that the years of your life may be many. I have taught you the way of wisdom; I have led you in the paths of uprightness. When you walk, your step will not be hampered, and if you run, you will not stumble. Keep hold of instruction; do not let go; guard her, for she is your life. Do not enter the path of the wicked, and do not walk in the way of the evil. Avoid it; do not go on it; turn away from it and pass on.

A father and mother have the responsibility to encourage their son to walk in "the paths of uprightness" and not in "the way of the evil." Now is the time to engage your son on critical issues like this, because the stakes are so high. These conversations will be critical to his growth as a man. They may even save his life.

Have you committed to being responsible for his moral and spiritual training?

Do you know what kind of man you want your son to become? Have you committed to being responsible for his moral and spiritual training? Are you involved—and will you stay involved—in your son's life? With these commitments in place, let the conversations begin.

4

Conversation #1:
Skill in Everyday Living

Many boys just do not know what to do when they are pursued by aggressive girls. Yet an even more troubling fact has become clear as I read through letters and e-mails from parents who are facing this issue: Many boys don't even see it as a problem. They welcome the attention. They are filled with curiosity and are excited about the opportunity to begin experimenting with sexual contact. Many of these boys are not prepared to face the pull of temptation. Being "wired" to embrace the lure of the moment, they naively believe they can extricate themselves whenever they choose.

But that's not likely, is it? Joe and Kathy certainly don't think so. And for good reason.

Seth, Joe and Kathy's seventeen-year-old son, was seduced by his twenty-one-year-old supervisor at the fast-food restaurant

> Even if a boy grows up in a home where he is regularly exposed to Christian teaching, that alone does not guarantee that he will make the right choices.

where he worked. Seth began sneaking out of the house, meeting the woman in her car, and driving to her apartment.

Joe and Kathy were already suspicious about the relationship because of texts they had read on Seth's cell phone. When they looked at the cell phone again a few weeks later, they could tell he had deleted dozens of texts. But they saw enough to piece together what was going on. Seth confessed that he had visited the woman a couple dozen times, but he claimed that they spent those nights playing video games. Eventually, he admitted the sexual relationship. He said he was in love.

It was obvious that the supervisor had pursued Seth and had set up their liaisons, but it was also obvious that Seth had put up no resistance.

Even if a boy grows up in a home where he is regularly exposed to Christian teaching, as Seth was, that alone does not guarantee that he will make the right choices. Hearing is not enough. That young man must *own* his beliefs and convictions. He must make the personal commitment to obey what Jesus Christ taught in the Gospels. Otherwise he is very much like the man Christ described in Matthew 7:26–27. "And everyone who hears these words of mine and does not do them will be like a foolish man who built his house on the sand. And the rain fell, and the floods came, and the winds blew and beat against that house, and it fell, and great was the fall of it."

Without the foundation of knowing *and obeying* the words of Jesus Christ, no boy—or girl or woman or man—will be able to withstand the rain, wind, and floods of a culture that continually tempts him to choose the desires of the flesh over obedience to Christ.

Timeless truths

As our sons moved into adolescence, one of the most important things I did was establish a standing weekly breakfast appointment with them. Teenage boys love food, so I used a hearty breakfast of donuts for bait. My goal was to get them into the Book of Proverbs and to get the Book of Proverbs *into* them. Sometimes we would read a few verses and stop and talk. Other times we would read the entire chapter. Each week, we would talk about one or two of the issues that Solomon, who wrote most of Proverbs, was passing on to his son. Some of the sessions were lively. At other times it felt like a dud. But we just kept pressing into the words of the wisest man who has ever lived.

One reason I like the Book of Proverbs is that it was written to help young men develop their own convictions where life and truth collide. If you are like I was when I started out my "Proverbs-donut study," you may be surprised to see how these timeless words, written several thousand years ago, are so relevant to what young men, as well as older men, face today.

The purpose of the Book of Proverbs is to encourage us to seek wisdom, which I define as "skill in everyday living." The words in this book help us to "know wisdom and instruction, to understand words of insight, to receive instruction in wise dealing, in righteousness, justice, and equity; to give prudence to the simple, knowledge and discretion to the youth" (Proverbs 1:2–4).

As I lead you through the first few conversations to have with your son, we're going to work through chapters 5 through 7 of Proverbs. The truths here will give your son a foundation for standing strong in a sexualized culture that will continually tempt him to abandon the way of wisdom. These truths will also help him develop a wholesome view of sexual attraction and understand God's purpose for sex.

As I mentioned in the previous chapter, Proverbs is full of godly instruction and wisdom from a father to his son. Proverbs 5 begins with the exhortation, "My son, be attentive to my wisdom; incline your ear to my understanding, that you may keep discretion, and your lips may guard knowledge" (Proverbs 5:1–2). In *The Message* (a modern paraphrase that I like because its words are potent), the father says his words will help the son "acquire a taste for good sense; what I tell you will keep you out of trouble."

> **My son, be attentive to my wisdom, incline your ear to my understanding, that you may keep discretion, and your lips may guard knowledge.**

It's important for your son to understand the need to listen to godly wisdom, true godly skill in everyday living. And it's critical for him to seek that wisdom from you. As children enter adolescence, they increasingly become dependent upon their friends. But on many issues, the advice of friends will be foolish.

Talking about real-life issues

Of course, if you want your son to listen to you, make sure that you are worthy of being heard. That means that you are following God yourself—that you are modeling a life of faith and obedience to Jesus Christ and His Word. You know what you believe, and you have determined the standards, boundaries, and convictions for your family. This also means that you are building a relationship with your son—that you are connected emotionally and affectionately. Your relationship with your son is like a bridge to his soul. If the bridge goes down or has never been built, he won't listen to you.

If your son is ten to twelve years old, the task is a bit easier because he will still listen to you more readily. Years ago, when I was leading a sixth-grade Sunday school class, I surveyed the kids and asked, "If you could ask your parents any question—but I would ask it for you, and then give you the answer later—what would it be?" Here are some of their questions:

"If I become pregnant before marriage, what would your reaction be?"

"Did you have sex before you were married?"

"How old will I be before I can kiss?"

"How old were you when you first had sex, and who was it with?"

"What qualities should the person I marry have?"

Isn't it interesting what our children have on their minds at that age? Fathers and mothers have a phenomenal opportunity to connect with their children over questions like these. By engaging your son in conversations over real-life issues, you can teach and influence him with biblical wisdom that will guide him and protect him.

In my mind there is no doubt, one of the best things I did with my sons was that Proverbs-donut study. I want to encourage you to get a copy of your favorite Bible and start your own study with your son. Use the discussion guide I have provided at the end of the next few chapters and begin the conversation. Over time, you will develop a connection with your son that will help him understand that he should listen to you when you talk about difficult issues like sex, purity, and aggressive girls.

TALK ABOUT IT

The goal of this conversation is to help your son understand the need to seek godly wisdom and where to find it. (Note: Make sure you and your son each have a copy of the Bible. If possible, use the same translation.)

1. Read Matthew 7:24–27. What do you think Jesus means when He says we need to *hear* His words and *do* them?

2. This scripture says that if we don't obey God's Word, our lives will be like a man who builds his house on sand. What do you think that means?

Suggestion: Take your son outside and show him the foundation of your house. Talk about what would happen to your house if it were built on sand.

3. Tell your son about a time in your life when you had to make a choice between obeying God's Word or following your own desire. Be as specific as you can in your description (What were you thinking and feeling? Why did you want to do it? What were you afraid of?) Then, tell him what choice you made and what the results or consequences were.

4. Ask your son if he would be willing to share a situation that he's facing right now. Or, if he's not facing a temptation right now, then ask him to share one from the past.

5. Read Proverbs 5:1–2. Explain that the Book of Proverbs contains practical advice that will give him wisdom and keep him out of trouble. The question for all of us who read these words is whether we will follow this advice and obey God's Word or whether we will be like the foolish man who built his house on sand.

6. Read 1 Corinthians 15:33. Ask: What do you think this verse means when it says that bad company ruins good morals?

7. Take turns telling about a time when you did what a friend said, and it turned out to be bad advice.

8. Read Proverbs 6:20–23. Talk about the need to follow the wisdom of parents. Explain that you understand what he's going through because you've been through similar things.

Note to Dad or Mom: I have given you more than enough questions here for your time with your son. Don't feel like you have to go through all of them. If your son starts talking and sharing about what's going on in his world, then just listen. Also, do not act like you are surprised or that you are judging him. Remember what it was like to be a teenager!

5

Conversation #2: The Big Test of Sexual Temptation

One of my favorite questions to ask men is, what's the most courageous thing you've ever done? During a recent radio interview, I asked the host that question. He instantly gave his answer, sharing that when he was fifteen years old, an "older" young lady of sixteen offered him a ride home after school. As she was driving, she took a detour and headed toward her house, saying, "My parents aren't going to be home for a long time. Why don't we hook up and have some fun?"

He went on to explain, "We were almost to her house . . . I was a virgin, and it was all so very tempting, but . . . I told her to turn around, and take me home." He continued, "Looking back on that decision, there's no question that remains the most courageous thing I've ever done in my life."

In Proverbs 5:3–14, we see what type of trouble my friend avoided that day:

> The lips of a seductive woman are oh so sweet, her soft words are oh so smooth. But it won't be long before she's gravel in your mouth, a pain in your gut, a wound in your heart. She's dancing down the primrose path to Death; she's headed straight for Hell and taking you with her. She hasn't a clue about Real Life, about who she is or where she's going.
>
> So, my friend, listen closely; don't treat my words casually. Keep your distance from such a woman; absolutely stay out of her neighborhood. You don't want to squander your wonderful life, to waste your precious life among the hardhearted. . . .
>
> You don't want to end your life full of regrets, nothing but sin and bones, saying, "Oh, why didn't I do what they told me? Why did I reject a disciplined life? . . . My life is ruined!" (MSG)

Depending on the Bible translation, the woman in this passage is called an adulterous woman, a forbidden woman, or a seductive woman. Many consider her to be a prostitute, but I find it interesting that her description applies to any woman—young or old—who sets out to seduce and entrap a man.

King Solomon provides clues for spotting her—her lips are sweet and "her soft words are oh so smooth." Your son needs to understand how aggressive girls will lure him with flattery, seductive behavior, what they wear (or don't wear), and that certain look in their eyes that he might find attractive but is anything but innocent. The advent of text messaging and social networking sites has compounded the problem, giving aggressive girls more ways to set the trap.

The challenge of helping your son avoid becoming ensnared by a sexually aggressive young lady is exacerbated today because of what is known as "hooking up." In the past, the temptation toward sexual involvement progressed from flirting, to a bit of a relationship, to a date or a series of dates—which for many led to intercourse. Today, however, "hook ups" have reversed the process. The modern girl thinks nothing of asking or luring a guy to have sex *before* they have much of a relationship. This generation views sex as little more than a handshake. Your son needs to understand that when a young man and woman give themselves to one another, they are engaging in the most intimate expression that a man and a woman can experience. This is why God exhorts us to save this expression until marriage. More on that later.

I don't think it is an accident that so much of Proverbs 5 through 7 focuses on the dangers of a seductive woman. How a young man handles *repeated* sexual temptation is one of the greatest tests of his life. A teenage boy fights the battle of lust every time he is tempted to look at pornography or to fantasize about a female rock star. And the fire of battle really intensifies if he is pursued by a girl who wants to sleep with him.

He needs to understand that this fight doesn't go away with age. The intensity of the battle may peak in the teen years, but he must be equipped for a war that will span his lifetime.

> **While protecting our sons, we should also pray for these girls.**

I do want to make one more observation from the Proverbs 5 passage, because I am moved by the sentence, "She hasn't a clue about Real Life, about who she is or where she's going." A girl like this may not understand why she is seeking affection, and she doesn't think about the consequences of her actions. So, while protecting our sons, we should have compassion and pray for these girls.

Joseph's test

Perhaps the clearest example in Scripture about resisting the advances of an aggressive woman is the story of Joseph. After being sold into slavery by his jealous brothers (Genesis 37), he ended up serving Potiphar, a high-ranking officer in Egypt.

Potiphar quickly recognized that God was with Joseph, so he put him in charge of his household and possessions.

An important part of Joseph's story is told in Genesis 39:6–10:

> Now Joseph was handsome in form and appearance. And after a time his master's wife cast her eyes on Joseph and said, "Lie with me." But he refused and said to his master's wife, "Behold, because of me my master has no concern about anything in the house, and he has put everything that he has in my charge. He is not greater in this house than I am, nor has he kept back anything from me except yourself, because you are his wife. How then can I do this great wickedness and sin against God?" And as she spoke to Joseph day after day, he would not listen to her, to lie beside her or to be with her.

This was a significant test for Joseph. By rejecting the relentless sexual advances of Potiphar's wife, his relationship with God grew stronger and stronger. And so, even when she falsely accused him of rape, causing Joseph some prison time, he recognized that God would continue to use him no matter what the circumstances. God blessed Joseph's obedience by using him to save an entire nation from starvation.

Your son needs to understand: God always takes note of obedience.

Most of your sons are not being pursued by someone's wife (although they may be when they are older). But think about what Joseph's legacy would have been if he'd succumbed to temptation, or how many lives would have been scarred if he'd failed. He passed the test, because he was prepared for it.

Is your son prepared? The temptations he faces are just as real, and there's no sure way of knowing what the consequences will be down the line.

A young man who is lured by this type of woman will pay a price if he gives in to the temptation. Our culture tells us that there is nothing wrong with teenagers exploring their sexuality. "How could something so pleasurable be a sin?" we are told. But sexual immorality catches up with him in the end. He will pay a big price in loss of respect, broken relationships, a lack of trust with his parents, the risk of sexually transmitted infections, and, most importantly, in his relationship with God. As Proverbs 6:27–29 (MSG) says, "Can you build a fire in your lap and not burn your pants? Can you walk barefoot on hot coals and not get blisters? It's the same when you have sex with your neighbor's wife: Touch her and you'll pay for it. No excuses."

On the other hand, the young man who learns how to resist temptation builds godly discipline and character that will serve him for life. Psalm 1 describes the man who heeds God's Word as "a tree planted by streams of water that yields its fruit in its season, and its leaf does not wither" (v. 3).

Isn't that what you want for your son?

TALK ABOUT IT

The goal of this conversation is to help your son truly understand that how he learns to handle sexual temptation now will prove to be one of the biggest tests of his life. A good number of these questions can be discussed by mom and/or dad, but a few of them are best discussed by a father and son. If that's not possible, then a mom must press into these discussions. (You may consider asking a man in your extended family or an influential man in your son's life to engage in these conversations.)

1. Start by telling your son about some of the sexual temptations you face on a regular basis. You can talk about the images you see or about some of the ways you might be tempted at work. Make it clear that sexual temptation is part of the everyday life of a man, and it's important to learn how to deal with it while he's young. This may seem over the top, but it's important for a young man to know how his dad and mom have experienced temptation.

2. Read Proverbs 5:3–6. Ask your son to describe the woman in this passage.

3. Have you encountered any girls who say they like you, or want to be your girlfriend, or want to have sex with you? Do you know about any girls like this? Have any of them come on to you? What did you do?

If he hasn't faced these things yet, he will.

Explain that in these conversations you're going to talk about how he should deal with sexual temptation and, specifically, how he should handle girls who pursue him. Explain that if he hasn't faced these things yet, he will.

4. Read Proverbs 5:7–14. What does this scripture say you should do with girls who try to seduce you? (Later, we'll talk about some practical ways to stay away from girls like this.)

5. What does this passage say will happen if we don't follow this advice?

6. Read Proverbs 5:21–23. What do you think it means when it says that our foolish decisions will trap us in a dead end (*The Message*)? When we do not obey God, how does that affect our relationship with Him? (If you can, tell a story from your life that illustrates this.)

7. Look at the story of Joseph and Potiphar's wife. (You may want to read Genesis 37–44 ahead of time and just tell him the story.)

Why do you think Potiphar's wife wanted to seduce Joseph?

Why do you think Joseph rejected her advances?

Discuss how God blessed Joseph for his obedience.

8. Explain to your son that over the next few years you will be having a number of discussions about sex, dating, and relating to girls. Make it clear that he is safe in discussing these things with you. Let him know that there is nothing he can share with you that will cause you to love him less.

6

Conversation #3:
The Great Gift of Sex

One of the myths of our culture is that God is down on sex.

When I interviewed pastor and author Joshua Harris on my radio program, *FamilyLife Today,* he said, "Isn't that how some people view the Christian perspective on sex—that the teaching in the Bible is really just a bunch of rules to try to keep us from enjoying sexuality? That's not true, and if you think that, you need to throw out that lie, because the truth is this: God created sex. It was He who made us with bodies that are able to experience physical pleasure. It was He who planted in us the desire for the opposite sex."

I absolutely agree. But there are conditions. Take a look at Proverbs 5:17–20:

Your spring water is for you and you only, not to be passed around among strangers.

Bless your fresh-flowing fountain! Enjoy the wife you married as a young man! Lovely as an angel, beautiful as a rose—don't ever quit taking delight in her body. Never take her love for granted! Why would you trade enduring intimacies for cheap thrills with a whore? for dalliance with a promiscuous stranger? (MSG)

God created sex, made it good, and made it for our enjoyment. But He reserves this gift for marriage. With the culture sending a barrage of murky messages about sex, your son *needs* to know what the Divine Designer had in mind when He created us with the capacity to enjoy sexual pleasure in marriage.

Sexual intercourse is more than a physical act. God made sex for procreation—to create children—but He also made it for pleasure. Case in point: Another translation of Proverbs 5:19 says, "Let her breasts fill you at all times with delight; be intoxicated always in her love." That's not *Playboy* 5:19; that's *Proverbs* 5:19. The Bible openly declares the delicious delight of sexual intimacy in marriage.

Sex is also designed to bind a husband and wife together emotionally and spiritually. In a profound and mysterious way they become "one flesh" (Genesis 2:24). This is a deep, satisfying intimacy reserved for marriage, and that is why the writer of Proverbs asks, "Why would you trade enduring intimacies for cheap thrills with a whore? for dalliance with a promiscuous stranger?"

Unfortunately, in our culture the idea of waiting for sex until marriage is generally regarded as unrealistic and old-fashioned. A 2011 Gallup Poll indicated that 60 percent of Americans believe sex between an unmarried man and woman is morally acceptable, with only 36 percent saying it was morally wrong.[1] Another study indicated that over 70 percent of unmarried singles who considered themselves religious had engaged in sex within the last year.[2] The boundaries have been moved. And the parents who are raising the girls your son goes to school with may not have even set boundaries.

Mark Gregston, who has worked with teenagers for more than thirty years, writes that he is amazed by the pressure teenagers feel to give in to promiscuity. "Kids today think of sex as something as natural to do—even at their age and out of wedlock—as breathing, exercising or eating ice cream. The kids I'm talking about are not the 'bad crowd'; they are teens, mostly from good Christian homes who were raised in the church.

> **God created sex, made it good, and made it for our enjoyment. But He reserves this gift for marriage.**

Yet they seem to compartmentalize morality between what's appropriate at home or church and what's okay to do with their friends."[3]

A young man who wants to protect his purity until he's married will face a long battle. He needs to understand that it's worth it to wait, and that the consequences of taking the wrong path are more severe than he has been led to believe. The scars will be with him for his entire lifetime.

Sex education needs to start early

As Barbara and I raised our two sons (and four daughters), we realized that we didn't want to leave it to the world to teach them about sex. We wanted to be the ones who taught them the basics of sex education, *and we wanted to teach them about God's perspective of sex—that it is sacred*. We began the process early, beginning at ages six and seven, with the basic discussions about the differences between male and females and how babies are made.

When your son is between ten and twelve, it is about to be "Game Time"—puberty is about to kick into gear. It is time to launch into some gritty conversations on topics like how his body is about to change and what that is all about; what sexual attraction is and how he should learn to manage his most important sex "organ"—his mind. He needs to understand what erections and wet dreams are all about. He must begin to comprehend his responsibility as a young man for protecting girls (physically, morally, and emotionally) and how he should relate to girls and respect them.

Incidentally, FamilyLife offers a great resource for these discussions. Passport2Purity® is a kit that completely guides you through a special weekend with your son or daughter and sets up discussions about issues they will confront in adolescence. It deals with puberty, peer pressure, dating, boundaries, and maintaining sexual purity. If you haven't taken your son through Passport2Purity, this is a must for any boy who is about to enter puberty.

As our sons moved through adolescence, we kept initiating conversations about maintaining their purity and innocence. But we wanted them to understand that Scripture calls us to much more than just virginity before marriage.

First Thessalonians 4:3–5, 7 tells us, "For this is the will of God, your sanctification: that you abstain from sexual immorality; that each one of you know how to control his own body in holiness and honor, not in the passion of lust like the Gentiles who do not know God . . . For God has not called us for impurity, but in holiness."

Having the right view of sex, God's view, is something a man needs to learn early, because it affects the spiritual trajectory of his life.

God wants the best for us

You will need to fight to keep your son focused on God's perspective on sex in this culture. He's not going to see a sacred view of sex on television, in the movies, or on the web. You will need to repeatedly challenge the world's view and contrast it with what we read in Scripture. Your son will need continual reminders of why God reserves sex for marriage; not just why he shouldn't partake of sex, but *why God wants him to wait*.

Joshua Harris told a story on *FamilyLife Today* about when he was twelve, and his family moved into a new home. He and his father visited the house, which was empty except for a box in the living room. Joshua saw that it was filled with pornographic magazines, and without thinking he reached toward them. His father stopped him. Joshua has never forgotten what he said next:

> Son, one day, God will give you a wife. And He wants you, when you're married, to delight in your wife's body. He wants you to see her as the most beautiful thing in the world. He wants you to feast your eyes on her naked body. Son, don't fill your mind with pictures and images

of other women that will compete with your wife, because you don't want to carry that into your marriage.

That is the type of guidance your son needs as you raise him to be a young man who follows God. He needs to understand that God is not toying with him by giving him urges that he shouldn't act on yet, and that you are not God's conniving gatekeeper. God has a great pleasure in store for him someday, and your desire is that he will be prepared to fully enjoy it with no regrets.

> **Son, don't fill your mind with pictures and images of other women that will compete with your wife.**

TALK ABOUT IT

The goal of this conversation is to help your son understand that God created sex to be enjoyed within the marriage relationship.

(Note: If your son is fourteen or younger, I suggest taking him through Passport2Purity and reading *So You Want to Be a Teenager* before having this discussion.)

1. Read Proverbs 5:17–20. What does this passage say about sex in marriage?

2. What does each of the following passages tell us about God's commands regarding sex?

   Matthew 15:19

   1 Corinthians 6:19

   1 Thessalonians 4:3–5, 7

3. Some people would say that God is being cruel by trying to keep us from enjoying something like sex. Why do you think God says that we should reserve sex for marriage?

4. Genesis 2:24 tells us, "Therefore a man shall leave his father and his mother and hold fast to his wife, and they shall become one flesh." A husband and wife becoming "one flesh" is more than just sexual intercourse. Sex brings about a special emotional and spiritual bond between a husband and wife. They are joined to each other. This bond is meant for marriage; it helps strengthen a married couple's commitment.

   Describe how you have found this to be so in your marriage.

5. When you consider how other people in our world look at sex—the things your friends might say, the things you see

on television—do you think they agree with God's desire to keep sex for marriage?

If you can, look at some examples in the media of how the world portrays sex, and show the contrast.

6. One of the major contributors to false images of sex that distorts what God wants for your son in marriage is pornography. Without getting into inappropriate details, share what, if any, impact pornography has had on your life, your spouse's life, and your marriage. Ask your son about how pornography has invaded his life. (For most young men today, it isn't a matter of *if* they've been exposed, but of *how much* they've seen.) Read Proverbs 4:23 and honestly talk about ways that he can safeguard his eyes and thus his heart.

7. Talk about the importance of standing for truth even when your friends don't believe as you do. Few people take the narrow and demanding road that requires sacrifice and discipline, while many people take the common road because it is easier and more comfortable. But God promises His blessings to those who obey His Word.

Conversation #4:
The Right Kind of Girl
Is Out There

When our youngest son turned thirteen, it was as if he had been discovered . . . by a swarm of female classmates. For several evenings, one after another called him on the phone. He was embarrassed by this newfound attention and a little put off by it. Barbara and I weren't wild about it either. When the phone rang the next evening, I was prepared. After I answered and the girl on the other end of the line asked to speak to my son, I told her that it was inappropriate for her and her friends to call like this, and I asked her to please stop. Now this was in the days before Twitter and cell phones, but these girls were somehow just as effectively connected. My message clearly got passed around, and the calls from the swarm stopped—instantly.

Many of you will encounter the problem of aggressive girls chasing your son when he is in junior high. Some of you will not. But I'm very confident that the older your son gets, the more likely he will face this issue. The challenge for you, as a parent, is that it may not be nearly as evident as the calls that suddenly started coming into our home.

Marcus was a junior in college. Committed to serving Christ, he hosted a Bible study in his dorm and was a member of the leadership team for a campus ministry. He developed a friendship with one of the women on this team, and at some point she began pursuing him. She texted several times a day, often asking him to meet her for meals.

"I'm very firm that I want to be the one to ask a girl out," Marcus explains. But in this case he finally consented to go on some casual dates, even though his gut told him something was wrong.

On one occasion, she suggested they watch a movie in his room. Sensing that she was scheming to be alone with him, Marcus asked a friend to join them. During the movie she fell asleep on the couch, and after the friend left she woke up. When Marcus told her it was time to go, she began acting sleepy and seductive. He knew what she wanted, and he was tempted, but he didn't give in.

Looking back, Marcus realizes that he was too passive. He didn't break off the relationship, but continued spending time with her and kept allowing himself to be put into situations where he would have to fight her off. When they were apart for the summer, she texted him every day, and he didn't respond. But when the school year started they saw each other again.

It was an inner battle. On one hand, he wanted to give in. "I knew I could turn to this girl in a time of loneliness, and I'd be guaranteed something," he says. But he would stop himself at the last minute. And finally, realizing he needed to break free of his passivity, he chose to break off the relationship.

> **Yet how many parents talk about this with their sons and prepare them for the inevitable?**

Learning what to watch out for

I would bet most fathers reading these words could tell a similar story from their days in high school, college, the military, or single adulthood. At some time, a man will encounter an aggressive woman. Many a man will give in. Many a man will fall.

Yet how many parents talk about this with their sons and prepare them for the inevitable?

Proverbs 7:6–22 is another insightful passage, because it helps a young man recognize the girls who are dangerous—those who may target him and bring him down through their seduction. It also highlights the dangers of passivity.

I want you to do more than just read this passage; I want you to take a close look at the process of how temptation gives birth to sin. In it, you will find specific descriptions of the women and the situations a young man should avoid. You may even want to underline or highlight those descriptions, so you can make them a part of the conversation with your son later.

> As I stood at the window of my house looking out through the shutters, watching the mindless crowd stroll by, I spotted a young man without any sense arriving at the corner of the street where she lived, then turning up the path to her house. It was dusk, the evening coming on, the darkness thickening into night. Just then, a woman met him—she'd been lying in wait for him, dressed to seduce him. Brazen and brash she was, restless and roaming . . .
>
> She threw her arms around him and kissed him, boldly took his arm and said, "I've got all the makings for a feast—today I made my offerings, my vows are all paid, so now I've come to find you, hoping to catch sight of your face—and here you are! I've spread fresh, clean

sheets on my bed, colorful imported linens. My bed is aromatic with spices and exotic fragrances. Come, let's make love all night, spend the night in ecstatic love-making! . . . Soon she has him eating out of her hand, bewitched by her honeyed speech. Before you know it, he's trotting behind her, like a calf led to the butcher shop . . . (MSG)

If you followed my suggestion, you found quite a few phrases to mark in this passage. Here are some that I found, along with some comments of what to talk about with your son.

- The young man "lacked sense." Two things are a possibility: either he had not been trained by his parents (because they were naive) to understand the seductive woman, or he hadn't listened. And as a result, he was truly clueless.

- He is where he shouldn't be—"at the corner of the street where she lived, then turning up the path to her house." A young man who wants to stay pure needs to stay far away from someone who wants to seduce him. (More on this in the next chapter.)

- He was out at night. People often do things at night—when they feel more "hidden"—that they would avoid during the day. They know they will not be caught as easily.

- She was "dressed to seduce him." Her clothes were designed to catch his eye by emphasizing her female attributes. Talk with your son about immodest dress and how to recognize it.

- She was "brazen and brash." She made it clear what she wanted from him, and she aggressively pursued him. Talk about the tactics girls may use and how to respond to them. (More on this in chapter 9.)

- She uses touch—in this case a suggestive kiss—as a lure. Tell your son about the power of touch and the electrifying effect even a seemingly innocent gesture can have on his body. Talk with him about the two kinds of kisses—the innocent peck on the cheek versus the passionate kiss that demands a sexual response.

- Her words were alluring, like honey. She made him feel important by letting him know she was waiting specifically for him. She described her bed and what she wanted to do in it. A boy needs to understand how a girl can manipulate him through her words—especially through flattery and sexual language.

- The woman was lying in wait for him. It's obvious from the entire passage that she set up a plan to entice him to her bed. Your son should know that some aggressive girls will lay elaborate plans and try to manipulate people and events in order to get what they want. Your son should listen up, not lay down! The sensuous power of a woman is one of the strongest forces on the planet . . . for good or evil.

While I was working on this chapter, a *FamilyLife Today* listener sent an e-mail that illustrates how some girls will devise a plan and lie in wait for a boy. Fourteen-year-old Seth was on his way to basketball practice when he saw a girl waiting for him outside the locker room. She had sent him notes saying she liked him, and she opened her arms for a hug, which they had done before. Then she grabbed his neck and sucked as hard as she could. Nobody would have known, but now he had a hickey on his neck, and he had to face his parents. Seth felt horrible and didn't want anything to do with the girl after that.

Your son needs to know that situations like this can happen in an instant.

Learning what to look for

Proverbs has much to say about the type of woman to avoid, so I find it interesting that the book ends with a long description of what to look *for* in a woman. "A good woman is hard to find," reads Proverbs 31:10, "and worth far more than diamonds" (MSG).

Reading through Proverbs 31:10–31, we see that a godly woman is trustworthy, generous, thrifty, hard-working, diligent, prudent, kind with her words, and much more. What a contrast to the forbidden woman described earlier.

In fact, this contrast is described in very plain terms in verse 30, "Charm is deceitful, and beauty is vain, but a woman who fears the LORD is to be praised." Above all, your son wants to look for a woman who fears God—who trusts Him with everything in her life, including her relationships.

Most of the letters I've received on this subject are from parents, but not all. I have also heard from some single females. Here is one comment from a twenty-year-old who read my online article about protecting sons from aggressive girls:

> I've tried to follow Christ and be an example for other girls. I've seen girls who have been aggressive and have called them on it. Most didn't know they were doing it! It shows how corrupt our world is and how much we are influenced by sinful things. I've also tried to be an encouragement to the guys around me. I've seen the effects of immodest dress. Guys need to know that there are good girls out there who are . . . faithfully sold out to Christ. It's sad to see so many men and women falter.

She concluded by quoting from Ephesians 6:10–11, which exhorts us, "Finally, be strong in the Lord and in the strength of his might. Put on the whole armor of God, that you may be able to stand against the schemes of the devil." Her battle to remain pure is just as intense as that of a young man.

I hope this letter encourages you and reminds you that there are many godly young women out there! Your son needs to know they are out there—they do exist—and they are worth waiting for.

TALK ABOUT IT

The goal of this conversation is to help your son understand the need to look for the right kind of girl.

1. Start by telling a story about the type of girls you dated. Tell about some good characteristics and some bad characteristics. If you had an experience with an aggressive girl, tell your son about it.

2. Read Proverbs 7:6–22. It's important for us to recognize the type of girl we should avoid. What are some of the things this passage says about girls like this?

   Look back at the summary I provided of the aggressive girl and the passive man (beginning on page 65). Go through the list, and discuss each point. With each description, ask your son if he has seen girls like this. Explain to him that he will encounter them as he grows older. It's also important to note that, while the intent of some of the girls he encounters is evil, other girls do not fully understand that what they are doing is wrong.

3. Now read through Proverbs 31:10–31. The writer of Proverbs spent a lot of time talking about the type of woman to avoid. But here he talks about the type of girl to look for in a wife. What are some of the things we find here about a good wife?

4. Tell your son about what you looked for in a wife. Talk about some of the ways your wife fits the description in Proverbs 31.

5. Ask your son to list some qualities that he would like in a wife. Then, look back over that list and perhaps suggest one or two qualities that you know he'll need. Close your time by praying for him to be a discerning young man. Pray, too, for the right young lady for him.

Conversation #5: The Gravitational Pull of Passivity

Dave and Sheila always prayed that when their children disobeyed them or God, they would get caught—that they wouldn't be able to deny it or lie their way out of it. Over the years, God answered those prayers. But they didn't expect that their son, Dustin, would be caught nearly having sex with his girlfriend.

Dustin, sixteen, had always been an obedient and trustworthy son, the kind of son who enjoyed time with his siblings, earned good grades at school, and eagerly participated in church activities. He wasn't the type to deceive his parents.

Emily was his first girlfriend. Dave and Sheila encouraged Dustin to join group activities with his friends instead of dating.

"We weren't against him being attracted to a girl," Sheila explains, "but we were against him pursuing a purposeless relationship with a girl."

Emily seemed like a nice girl, kind of shy and not overly aggressive. But behind the scenes she began maneuvering to persuade Dustin to sneak out of his house at night. At first he refused, but then he decided to try it. He rode his bike three miles at night to meet Emily in her family's motor home, which was parked next to their house.

At first, they just watched movies together, but then the kissing started. They never went all the way, but they would have if Emily's father hadn't caught them one night.

Dave and Sheila were devastated. It was the last thing they expected from Dustin. And what I find interesting is that after his parents forced him to break off the relationship, Dustin began to see clearly what had happened. He had been dazzled and blinded by Emily, and once he put some distance between them, he began to understand how it had happened—how Emily had manipulated him and how he had just gone along with it. He was shocked at how easy it had been to become ensnared.

Relational passivity

Perhaps you've noticed a common pattern in the stories I've been sharing: *aggressive girl pursues passive boy*. The girl initiates the relationship and presses the boy for sexual intimacy, and he puts up little or no resistance.

That same pattern holds true in the passages I've quoted from Proverbs. The writer of Proverbs paints several vivid pictures of seductive, aggressive women. And in each case, the young man was passive, allowing himself to be seduced.

> **We weren't against him being attracted to a girl, but we were against him pursuing a purposeless relationship with a girl.**

Growing up in our culture, one of your son's greatest challenges will be to reject this relational passivity. This is a critical step to his growth as a man. Scripture makes it clear that God calls on men to assume a leadership role in relationships, particularly in marriage, as well as in the culture and in the church. I don't have the space in this book to develop this theme as thoroughly as I would like, but let me highlight one passage that may be familiar to you, Ephesians 5:25, 33:

> Husbands, love your wives, as Christ loved the church
> and gave himself up for her . . . let each one of you

love his wife as himself, and let the wife see that she respects her husband.

God does not call husbands to a selfish, lording type of leadership. Instead, He commands them to love their wives, "as Christ loved the church and gave himself up for her." This is a leadership marked by love, servanthood, and self-denial. Throughout His earthly life Christ served others, and in His death He went to the cross on behalf of the church; He gave His life for those He loved. These are not acts of passivity but of heroic love.

If we allow young men to be lazy and passive in their early years, they will not be ready for the self-denial and sacrifice they will need when they are married. Their relationships with the opposite sex during junior high, high school, college, and beyond are a perfect training ground, providing opportunities to learn how to do two things that are crucial to manhood: (1) step away from temptation and (2) step up to do what's right.

Step away

Proverbs 7:24–27 highlights one the most important ways for a son to reject passivity:

> So, friends, listen to me, take these words of mine most seriously. Don't fool around with a woman like that; don't even stroll through her neighborhood. Countless

victims come under her spell; she's the death of many a poor man. She runs a halfway house to hell, fits you out with a shroud and a coffin. (MSG)

Your son should understand that he needs to step away from dangerous women and dangerous situations. It is a lesson he will apply for the remainder of his life.

Other scriptures back up this idea. Proverbs 22:3 says, "A prudent person sees trouble coming and ducks; a simpleton walks in blindly and is clobbered" (MSG). Second Timothy 2:22 implores us to "flee youthful lusts" (NASB). And the words of Matthew 5:28–30 are particularly graphic:

> "But I say to you that everyone who looks at a woman with lustful intent has already committed adultery with her in his heart. If your right eye causes you to sin, tear it out and throw it away. For it is better that you lose one of your members than that your whole body be thrown into hell. And if your right hand causes you to sin, cut it off and throw it away. For it is better that you lose one of your members than that your whole body go into hell."

Our sons need to understand that when they see temptation coming, they should run from it! If they allow themselves to go near it, they might become trapped.

> **Our sons need to understand that when they see temptation coming, they should run from it!**

For your son, fleeing youthful lusts will mean stepping away from girls (and not hanging out with them) who throw themselves at him and avoiding situations where he will be alone with a girl. And if he does find himself in such a situation, it means getting out of it immediately.

Your son may have to learn the need to flee aggressive girls even younger than you would have hoped. Here's what one parent told me in an e-mail:

My son is a fourth grader. I am amazed at the stories he has come home with, starting in second grade. Girls seem to be driven to aggression when it comes to boys. They desire to dominate. They form packs and chase the boys at recess, trying to hold them down and kiss them or sometimes just scratch them. . . . Does he fight back? . . . We feel that boys should protect girls, not fight them! Well, we gave him the advice Joseph used against Potiphar's wife: Run! He might become quite a track star from all the running he's been doing.

Fleeing youthful lusts also means remaining pure in what your son allows himself to look at. When he is confronted with opportunities to view pornography, he needs to know in advance what he's going to do; he should immediately turn away. This will mean avoiding any hint of pornography on the Internet and resisting pressure from friends who show him pictures, magazines, or websites. The same goes for music, television shows, or movies that feed his lust and lead him to think of girls in the wrong way.

As a parent I want to make sure you hear me on this one: Pornography is a setup for a boy to be seduced by a girl. The fantasy of porn *will* make your son easy prey for a *real* seductive girl.

He will need your help to identify these potential traps, and he will need you to help him set boundaries, so he can avoid them as much as possible. For example, we didn't encourage dating in junior high or high school; and when our children did have a date to the prom, they went with other couples in a group situation. Some might call this *controlling*, but it's not. It's *protecting*. And that's part of our job as parents. Teenagers need healthy accountability. (I'll talk more about boundaries in the next chapter.)

Step up

In addition to stepping away from temptation, a young man must also learn to step up and do what's right. When it comes to training your son on how to relate to girls, here are a few themes to emphasize:

- *Take responsibility for initiating relationships.* When you feel your son is ready to begin relating to girls, encourage him to set up group activities, preferably at your home. Also, encourage him to be the one who calls a girl to ask her out on a date, rather than vice versa.

- *Treat girls with dignity and respect.* This training can begin at an early age by teaching him how to show common courtesies toward his mother and sisters—things like opening doors and helping bring in groceries and heavy loads from the car. It continues when your son is a teenager and is tempted to use his strength and size to intimidate his mother; you need to step in and remind him to treat her with respect.

- *Be the moral leader when he is with girls.* Train him to keep his hands off girls and to establish these boundaries from the outset on his dates. He should treat each girl with the knowledge that someday she will become somebody's wife.

- *Protect the opposite sex.* As the physically stronger sex, men are called to a role of protecting their families. I remember when our kids were teenagers and my daughter Ashley worked at a pizza parlor and got off late one night. Her brother Benjamin was concerned that it was dangerous, so he went to pick her up. I put my arm around him and said, "Son, I just want to tell you how proud I am of you initiating that toward your sister." (By the way, an occasional "attaboy" will go a long way with your son. Be as attentive to his right choices as you are to his wrong ones, and be ready to pounce with affirmation.)

Finally, encourage your son to step up to pursue a relationship with Christ wholeheartedly. Even when he blows it, he can turn to God for forgiveness, grace, and a hope for his future.

I'm glad to say that Dustin's story (from the beginning of this chapter) has a good ending. You could say that the experience woke Dustin up. All those lessons and exhortations from his parents and from his pastors at church began to hit home. Fortunately for Dustin, he had parents who loved him despite his deceit. Yes, they were disappointed, but the grace and forgiveness they gave him ultimately resulted in his repentance. He confessed his sins, accepted his parents' discipline, and began spending time developing his relationship with God.

> **I am so thankful to God for loving us so much that He disciplines us.**

"He is now on fire for the Lord," Sheila says. "He had true repentance, and it was painful and hard, but beautiful. I truly believe this experience has changed his life forever. I am so thankful to God for loving us so much that He disciplines us."

TALK ABOUT IT

The goal of this conversation is to encourage your son to reject passivity in his relationships by stepping away from temptation and stepping up to embrace manly responsibility.

1. Read Proverbs 7:6–9. We've been talking a lot about protecting ourselves from dangerous women. As we've looked at the young man in these passages and at the temptations he faces, how would you describe him? What type of young man is he?

   This is not the type of man who is actively looking for a good woman and courting her. He's just sitting back and allowing himself to be swept along by this woman. He's being passive.

   In the past, a young man was expected to be the initiator in a relationship with a girl. Now, more and more boys are being passive and letting the girls make the first move. Your goal is to help your son grow into a man who is the initiator—the leader—in his relationships with women.

2. Imagine that there is a zoo near your school. One day the principal comes on the intercom and says, "We've just received a report that two large tigers have escaped from the zoo. These are dangerous animals—they already injured several people—and until they are caught, we need to have every student and teacher stay in their room." Then, sure enough, you hear the sound of the tigers. They're inside the building, walking down the hall. One of your friends says, "I've seen these tigers several times at the zoo, and they looked pretty tame to me. I don't see why everyone is so scared. I think we can take care of this problem ourselves." So he heads toward the door and is about to open it.

What would you do? (A) let your friend open the door and possibly let the tigers in? or, (B) tackle him, and get some of the other students to sit on him so that he can't open the door?

How would you apply this story to you observing a friend who was doing something with the opposite sex that was harmful or dangerous to him?

3. In our last conversation, we talked about some of the characteristics of girls who want to cause harm. Now read Proverbs 5:8 and 7:24–27. What do these verses say we should do whenever we are tempted by a woman like this?

This is the first step toward rejecting passivity in our relationships with women. We should take action by staying away from dangerous women and dangerous situations.

4. Second Timothy 2:22 tells us, "Now flee from youthful lusts." What do you think it means to flee from youthful lusts? What are some ways you can apply this in your life right now?

We should actively move in the other way when faced with something that would inflame lust. This means staying away from pornography. It means avoiding television shows that cause you to look with lust on a woman. It means not spending time with a girl who is trying to seduce you. It means not allowing your eyes and thoughts to linger on the physical attributes of a beautiful girl.

5. Now, let's look at some verses that talk about how a man should relate to a woman. Read Ephesians 5:25, 33.

What do you think it means when it calls a husband to love his wife as Christ loved the church? What kind of love is that?

6. These verses specifically talk about a man and a woman who are married. But from these principles, what can we

learn about how a single young man should relate to a single young woman?

A young man should treat women with love, respect, and dignity. He should look out for their interests rather than his own. He should initiate the relationship, as Christ initiates with us. He should be the moral leader when he is with girls, establishing and enforcing physical boundaries. And he should step up to protect the opposite sex.

For further reading and discussion with your son, I'd suggest that you get a copy of my book *Stepping Up: A Call to Courageous Manhood* and read it together. This would create further discussion around the subject of how real men step up to responsibility.

Conversation #6:
The Safety Zone

When our oldest, Ashley, entered her teenage years, it was unusual for any teen to have a cell phone; but by the time my youngest daughter, Laura, graduated from high school in 2003, it was unusual for someone her age *not* to have one. By 2009, about 75 percent of teens had cell phones, and most of them received their first while in middle school. Welcome to the "Screen Generation." Computer tablets, like the iPad, now sell faster than laptop computers and are the new textbook for education. The convenience is great—I have one myself—but I am also concerned that we may have opened up a new compartment in Pandora's box.[1]

The advances in personal technology and the growing popularity of electronic gadgets have made it difficult for parents to keep up with how their children are being affected. Parents usually give cell phones to children fourteen or younger because of a concern for safety; a cell phone helps parents monitor where their children are, and it allows the kids to call in an emergency. But without proper boundaries, these devices can lead to all kinds of problems and temptations for kids, especially when they are in middle school or younger.

What rules should parents set? When should a child even get his first cell phone? What about texting? What are the limits? Do moms and dads have access to text messages? And with the advent of schools using electronic tablets for education, young people have powerful communication devices that make a good old-fashioned telephone look like a wimp.

The current tool of choice for pursuing and seducing boys is the text message.

Reading through some of the e-mails I have received, it's obvious that *the current tool of choice for pursuing and seducing boys is the text message.* Here's a typical story: One parent wrote that her son had been given a cell phone in eighth grade. At a retreat, he met a girl who was a junior in high school who began sending him messages like, "I can't believe u r only an 8th grader! U look so much older!" and "I can't wait til u r in high school next year!" and "U r such a hottie!" Fortunately, this parent had set up some rules about cell phone use, and one was that she and her husband would look at his text messages at any time they wished. This allowed them to address the problem quickly.

"U r such a hottie!"

Cell phone use is just one area where parents need to be on guard. Boundaries need to be set for the use of tablets, computers, and in many other areas where our children are vulnerable.

The value of boundaries

Setting boundaries for your children's safety is not new to you; this is something you've been doing for years. You taught them not to cross a street before looking both directions. You did not allow them to accept rides from strangers. You warned them not to touch hot stoves or electrical outlets. You monitored the television shows and movies they viewed. However, as your children grow it becomes more of a challenge to establish and enforce new boundaries for new situations. But these boundaries are just as important as you finish the job of raising your children.

As your son moves into the preteen and teen years and his independence is on the rise, you may be tempted to disengage and shrink back. You may feel that your role as protector is mostly behind you. Not so. Your son needs your help—your boundaries—to keep him safe. Here are a few areas to consider:

Spending time with friends

You need to monitor your son's friendships to ensure that he spends time with people who are a positive influence. At some point, he'll likely have friends who ridicule the standards you set at home and will encourage him to deceive you and rebel. Don't relinquish your role in your son's relationships. As Barbara and I wrote in our book, *Parenting Today's Adolescent*:

> You are the parent. Realize that maintaining control of those who influence your children is within the bounds of your authority as a parent. As friendships begin to take shape, steer your children in the direction of positive peer pressure and away from negative influences. We have made it difficult for our children to spend time with friends who do not provide the kind of influence we desire. In certain cases, we've even declared certain friends off limits.[2]

Also, let your son know that you will be checking up to make sure he goes where he says he's going. If he's visiting a friend, especially one you are unfamiliar with, contact the parents to confirm. Keep in mind that many kids report they first began experimenting with drugs, alcohol, pornography, or sex when visiting friends overnight. Consider hosting events yourself so you can get to know his friends. There's an added benefit to this: many kids appreciate it when adults show a genuine interest in them. You might end up being one of the "cool" parents or, more importantly, get the opportunity to influence the next generation.

Establishing this type of accountability will also help you protect your son's innocence and enable you to evaluate the girls who come into his life.

Girls asking him out

Many of us grew up in an era where boys were expected to call girls to ask them out, and girls were usually taught by parents not to call boys. That rule is long gone. One mother was checking her thirteen-year-old daughter's text messages and saw that she was plotting with a friend to find the number of a boy she liked. The mother engaged her in a conversation around her pursuit of this young man. Ultimately, the mom explained why she didn't like her pursuing a boy. The daughter's response was, "Mom, this is a new day."

It is indeed a new day. However, as a parent you are still on duty—your God-given duty.

In the last chapter, I encouraged you to teach and train your son how to initiate in relationships. When he's ready for a relationship with a girl, encourage him to be the one who makes the call.

Internet and social networking

Many of you would be shocked at what young teens are posting on their personal online pages. One parent wrote:

> My eighth-grade son showed us his account, and we were amazed by the aggressive notes from girls that followed. Mood settings said things like "horny," "excited," and "naughty." We removed his account and let him know that "nice girls" don't solicit men or advertise inappropriately with their words, dress, or actions.

Another wrote:

> The talk and photos were like something from *Playboy*. I refused to let my twelve-year-old son have access. Freshman girls verbally seducing boys online and seeing nothing wrong with it, is just unbelievable. It's rampant, and the seductive pictures are disgusting.

I have three suggestions for you to consider here:

1. Do not allow your son (or daughter) to use a computer behind a closed door. Put the family computer in a common space where everyone can see it. You will avoid a lot of problems with this one simple rule. You may even want to install some kind of monitoring software. Remember,

the nature of adolescence is foolishness, deception, and hiding.

2. Do not allow your son (or daughter) to have an account on a social networking site until he is at least thirteen, and depending upon the maturity of the child, even later. In fact, Facebook officially does not allow children to have an account until they turn thirteen, but many parents send the wrong signal by allowing their children to disobey Facebook's rule.

> **Remember, the nature of adolescence is foolishness, deception, and hiding.**

3. Let your kids know you have full access to everything they do online, including e-mail and social networking accounts. When you do give your child the responsibility of getting involved in social media, create the expectation that you will be a "friend" and will have access to what's taking place on their page. I would suggest that initially you know the user name and password for all their social media and e-mail accounts. Take time to explain that social media and privacy are not their personal rights as an American. The phone, tablet, and computer are privileges to be earned . . . and potentially lost.

You may agree or disagree with what I am recommending, but it is imperative that as parents *you* decide what your boundaries will be in these areas. If you don't draw some lines and establish boundaries, then it is very likely that the culture and your son's peers will take your son to places and relationships that you don't want him to go.

The goal is to be intentional and engaged. As a parent, you need to monitor your son without hovering. I know of one father who gets a daily digital snapshot of his son's communication from his cell phone, tablet, and computer. On one occasion, a minor but inappropriate message was sent to him by a girl. Rather than confront the situation, the father intentionally waited and watched where the communication was headed. He later caught his son lying to him and was able to confront the situation without revealing all that he knew from monitoring his messages.

Many of these rules can become legalistic and stifling to a teen and actually encourage him to rebel. There is a careful tension in raising teens where the relational bridge stays in place, while at the same time you are driving all kinds of truth, convictions, and boundaries into his life. Parenting is an art, not an exact science.

Being alone with a girl

Another important boundary that you need to decide on is at what point you are willing to allow your son to be alone with a girl in a car, taking a walk, at a party, or in other settings. What lines will you draw to protect your son? Teach him to avoid situations where he would be alone, especially in the dark and behind closed doors. And let him know that an aggressive girl will look for ways to manipulate him so she can be alone with him.

A teenage young man may push back saying, "I don't feel like you trust me!" To which I would say, "I don't trust myself as a married man with a woman (who isn't my wife) alone . . . why should I trust you!?"

Family involvement

If your son shows interest in a particular girl, and you have determined he's old enough to pursue the relationship, let him know that you want to get to know her and her family. Invite her to dinner with your family. These kinds of relationships shouldn't be off limits to you as a parent or outside the protection of your family.

Cell phones

This may be the most difficult area of all to monitor, because cell phones are now so entrenched in our culture. Here are a few suggestions:

1. Determine as parents when your son will be allowed to have his own cell phone. Your son may try to make you feel like having one is an inalienable right. But as you know, it's a privilege that should be enjoyed by a young man who has demonstrated that he is responsible and mature enough to be trusted. You could even build up to the day when you "present" him with his phone, so that he values it as something he's earned and as a privilege that can be revoked.

2. Let him know that he will be fully accountable to you in how he uses his phone. For example, make sure he understands that

   - as the parent you are "allowed" to look at his phone whenever you wish and that you can also access call and texting records from your cellular carrier's online records;

   - initially, he will not be permitted to use the phone behind closed doors or after a certain hour; and

- if you find inappropriate messages on the phone, you will contact the person who sent them. If they continue, you will contact this person's parents.

3. Remind him that a cell phone is a privilege that can be taken away at any time. Cell phones are so important to teenagers that they provide a good discipline opportunity. If he doesn't follow your rules, take away his cell phone privileges for a period of time.

The value of accountability

I realize that by setting certain boundaries, you may be perceived as the strictest parents on earth. Your son will probably let you know that your rules are unfair. Please do not abdicate your parental responsibilities. Not only are you protecting your son, but you are also helping him understand the value of accountability, a scriptural principle that tells us to be "submitting to one another out of reverence for Christ" (Ephesians 5:21). This means choosing to submit our life to the scrutiny of another person in order to gain spiritual strength, growth, and balance.

Most teenage boys will resist accountability.

Most teenage boys will resist accountability. As his parents, you need to help him understand that it is a great defense against the temptations of the world, something that will serve him well all the days of his life.

TALK ABOUT IT

The purpose of this conversation is to emphasize the safety that boundaries and accountability offer.

Note: This conversation will require some advance preparation. First, you need to determine the boundaries that you are implementing for your son. Go through the topics discussed in this chapter and, along with your spouse, write down the boundaries you are establishing (or have established already). Be prepared to talk about these with your son.

1. Before this conversation, think about your community, and note some of the "boundaries" that are placed at various places as protection. Examples may be the fences that keep cows and horses from escaping their pasture, a yard fence that keeps children safe from traffic, the fences around a jail or prison, or the guardrails on a bridge that allow for scenic driving without plunging to a watery death.

Take your son out to eat. While driving to the restaurant, go by the locations you have chosen, and at each one ask questions like: Why do you think the owners of this property put up this boundary? Who does this boundary protect? What would happen if this boundary wasn't here?

Continue the conversation over dinner.

2. Our first few conversations were taken from the Book of Proverbs. What are some of the main things you remember from our times together?

3. Talk about some of the boundaries that you have established (or are establishing now) to protect your son. Discuss why it is good to have rules and boundaries. Consider asking him to make a list of why he feels that boundaries are helpful.

4. Talk through the list of boundaries that are designed to protect him in the areas of sex, purity, and aggressive girls. For each one, explain why you are implementing this boundary and how it will help protect him. Give him an opportunity to ask questions, so he understands what is expected of him.

5. Discuss what accountability is and why it's important, not only now but for his entire life. Share with your son a friend to whom you are accountable. Share how you are accountable and why that relationship and accountability are so important to you.

10

Conversation #7:
The Game Plan

There are good coaches, and there are bad coaches. You've probably experienced some of both.

A good coach knows how to motivate and encourage his players. He knows how to get the best out of them. Most importantly, he is a teacher; he knows how to play the game, and he knows how to teach those skills to his players.

A youth baseball coach will work with each of his players to show them the basics of throwing, fielding, hitting, and baserunning. He will teach them the basics of defense—what base to throw to, when to tag a runner or step on a base for an out, and how to turn a double play. And a quality coach will go even further. He will teach them what to do in different situations. If you're playing third base and the opposing team has runners at first and second with one out, and the batter hits a grounder

> **Your goal is to build and shape your son's convictions so that, when faced with situations that tempt him to compromise his faith and his sexual purity, he will know how to respond.**

straight to you, what do you do? What if the ground ball goes to the pitcher? What if it's a single to left field or a pop fly to first base?

Over and over, the coach will drill his players in the "what if?" situations they may face during a game, so that when those situations come up, *the players will know what to do.*

I think one of the problems with teenagers today is that they lack this type of training. They haven't been taught to decide in advance what to do with the choices they will face.

Think of yourself as a coach. You know what types of challenges your children will face during the adolescent years; you've been through them yourself. You know that friends will tempt them, for example, to drink or to take drugs. They will be tempted to cheat and steal and lie, to look at pornography, and to have sex. They will be faced with choices about how to deal with a bully or how to react when a fight breaks out at school. You can help coach them through these situations by teaching and training them in advance in how to make the right choices.

Many of the e-mails I've received about aggressive girls have mentioned specific situations boys have faced. For example:

My son was hanging out with some of his buddies when a girlfriend of one of the other guys and some of her friends stopped over. They were giggling about having shopped at Victoria's Secret. One of them pulled a thong out of her bag to show my son. He just smiled, embarrassed. A while later, while Joe was half-laying on the couch, trying to play video games, the girl came and laid on top of him!

Your goal is to build and shape your son's convictions so that, when faced with situations that tempt him to compromise his faith and his sexual purity, he will know how to respond. I like the challenge of 1 Peter 1:13–16, which tells us:

Therefore, preparing your minds for action, and being sober-minded, set your hope fully on the grace that will be brought to you at the revelation of Jesus Christ. As obedient children, do not be conformed to the passions of your former ignorance, but as he who called you is holy, you also be holy in all your conduct, since it is written, "You shall be holy, for I am holy."

As parents, you can help your son prepare his mind for action and learn how to conform to the holiness of Christ and not the passions that seek to dominate his life. Begin to think of yourself as a "life coach," training him how to make the right choices.

An offensive game plan: three strategic scriptures

None of this training will work unless your son understands that it is possible to withstand temptation and to deal with difficult situations involving aggressive girls. On one hand, at home he hears about the values of abstaining from sex and withstanding temptation. On the other hand, he lives in a culture where these values are rarely modeled and frequently undermined. Very few people are telling your son that he does not have to give in to his passions—that it is possible to withstand the lure of sexually aggressive girls.

A good starting point is to work with him to memorize key scriptures and to understand the principles they teach. Help your son internalize these truths:

1. *The Scriptures can help him keep his way pure.* Psalm 119:9–11 tells us, "How can a young man keep his way pure? By guarding it according to your word. With my whole heart I seek you; let me not wander from your commandments! I have stored up your word in my heart, that I might not sin against you."

2. *He can withstand any temptation.* First Corinthians 10:13 tells us, "No temptation has overtaken you that is not common to man. God is faithful, and he will not let you be tempted beyond your ability, but with the temptation he will also provide the way of escape, that you may be able to endure it."

3. *God gives courage to face our battles.* Joshua 1:7–9 reads, "Only be strong and very courageous, being careful to do according to all the law that Moses my servant commanded you. Do not turn from it to the right hand or to the left, that you may have good success wherever you go. This Book of the Law shall not depart from your mouth, but you shall meditate on it day and night, so that you may be careful to do according to all that is written in it. For then you will make your way prosperous, and then you will have good success. Have I not commanded you? Be strong and courageous. Do not be frightened, and do not be dismayed, for the LORD your God is with you wherever you go."

Your son's faith will correspond to how well he understands and obeys God's Word. Memorizing key passages like these and others will help him draw upon God's power in times of temptation.

Decide in advance

As our children approached adolescence, Barbara and I began playing the "Decide in Advance" game with them. We would develop a list of situations they would likely face and then talk about what choices they should make. For example, "You are fifteen and at a friend's house. Your friend pulls a couple of beers out of the refrigerator. Nobody else is at home. What would you do?"

We would role play the situation, and we'd do it for a number of different situations—drugs, smoking, stealing, watching inappropriate movies, etc. We would talk to our sons about what to do if friends showed them pornography, or if a group of guys were talking about girls in a crude way, or if friends started making fun of them because they were still virgins.

In the "Talk About It" section at the end of this chapter, you will find some situations to discuss with your son about dealing with aggressive girls along with some suggestions on points to emphasize with him. As you play the "Decide in Advance" game, be sure to ask him about other situations he may be facing, and role play these as well.

Undoubtedly, your child will also tell you about situations where he has failed to make the right choice. In fact, when faced with this level of temptation, some failure should be expected.

(Again, remember your own battle with the various temptations you still face; nobody wins every time.) When failure occurs, accept him, love on him, and remind him of God's love and grace. These are great opportunities to teach him to think rightly about God's love and forgiveness. And remind him that there is nothing he can do that can cause you to love him less.

> **When failure occurs, accept him, love on him, and remind him of God's love and grace.**

Then help him think through what he should have done. As you deal with these failures, remember that some good testing of convictions is exactly what you want to occur when your son is still at home—where you can demonstrate forgiveness, as well as guide, correct, and instruct him. Although discipline may be required, be sure to balance it with forgiveness and encouragement. Being a young person is very challenging. He needs to know you're on his side.

Just as important, praise your son when he does well. When my sons made good choices, I went crazy . . . "Way to go! Give me a high five!" Your affirmation will offset the negative feedback he receives from friends or from the girl he rejects in his effort to remain pure. Don't miss this opportunity to applaud your son as you coach and train him. He will draw upon this training for his entire life.

TALK ABOUT IT

The goal of this conversation is to help your son begin memorizing some key biblical passages about sexual purity and to discuss some "Decide in Advance" situations involving aggressive girls. It may not be possible to do this all in one conversation.

1. Talk about the need for training in many areas of our lives. If he's interested in sports, talk about the need to learn specific skills and how to apply those skills in specific situations. If he's not interested in sports, try the subject of driving. When learning to drive, it's important to learn things like how to operate a car, how to make turns, and how to stay within your lane. It's important to know and understand the laws that govern the roads and to prepare for situations he might encounter while behind the wheel.

   Explain to your son that training in dealing with aggressive girls needs to involve the same type of discussions where you talk about what to do in potential situations.

2. Talk about the importance of having the right mindset as he thinks about the temptations he faces. If he thinks it is impossible to turn away from a temptation, then he will have no chance of withstanding it. But knowing ahead of

time that God can give him the strength to withstand temptation will make all the difference. He doesn't have to fail.

For each of the following passages, ask your son what he thinks it means, and then discuss the main point:

- Psalm 119:9–11: "How can a young man keep his way pure? By guarding it according to your word. With my whole heart I seek you; let me not wander from your commandments! I have stored up your word in my heart, that I might not sin against you." (God's Word can help you keep your way pure.)

- 1 Corinthians 10:13: "No temptation has overtaken you that is not common to man. God is faithful, and he will not let you be tempted beyond your ability, but with the temptation he will also provide the way of escape, that you may be able to endure it." (You can withstand any temptation.)

- Joshua 1:7–9: "Only be strong and very courageous, being careful to do according to all the law that Moses my servant commanded you. Do not turn from it to the right hand or to the left, that you may have good success wherever you go. This Book of the Law shall not depart from your mouth, but you shall meditate on it day and night, so that you may be careful to do according to all that is written in it. For then you will make your way prosperous, and then you will have good success. Have I not commanded you? Be strong and courageous. Do not be frightened, and do not be dismayed, for the LORD your God is with you wherever you go." (God gives us courage to face our battles; obeying His Word will bring success.)

3. Following are a number of "Decide in Advance" scenarios. For each, read the text and ask, "What do you think you should do in a situation like this?" Discuss some possible solutions. (I have included some suggestions.)

Situation #1: You meet a girl, and she immediately begins sending you notes or text messages telling you that she likes you and wants to see you again. She does this several times a day, and you're not interested. (Also ask, "What would you do if you are interested, and she keeps sending notes?")

Suggestion: Text her and say that you are not interested in developing a relationship with her, and ask her to stop sending you messages. If she continues, let your parents know, and ask them to text her. If she still doesn't stop, ask them to contact her parents.

If he likes her, and she is really aggressive, suggest that as good as it feels to have her pursuing him, to come talk to you about it and discuss what is healthy and appropriate and what isn't.

Situation #2: You are trading text messages with a girl that you like, and after a while the messages start becoming more suggestive. She tells you that she thinks you're really hot, and she begins to say she'd like to have sex with you. She also to suggests that you sneak away at night and meet her.

Suggestion: Let your parents know right away that a girl has become too aggressive in her approach to you. Tell the girl, in text and in person if possible, to stop. Block her number. If she tries to contact you by some other means, ask your parents to contact her. If she still continues, your parents should contact her parents.

Situation #3: When you walk past a certain group of girls at school in the hallway, they keep making sexual comments and grabbing your butt.

Suggestion: Get your rear in gear, and get out of there! If it happens again, tell a teacher or administrator.

Situation #4: A girl sends you a suggestive photo of herself. Or, someone forwards you a photo that is inappropriate.

Suggestion: This is a serious situation—not only is the girl becoming overly aggressive, but photos like this are sometimes classified as child pornography and can be considered a crime. First, tell your parents that you received this photo so they know what has happened. Second, immediately reply, "Never send me anything like that again!" so you have an electronic record of refusal. You might even take a picture or screen shot of your reply. Then, immediately erase the photo from your phone. It's very important that you do not forward the photo or show the phone to anyone else—some kids in situations like this have been charged with spreading child pornography. Next, make sure your parents contact her parents, so she is not getting herself and any other recipient of those photos in deeper trouble.

Situation #5: A girl begins sitting next to you every day during lunch in the school cafeteria. She seems nice, but you're not interested in a relationship with her.

Suggestion: In a situation like this, the girl may not be acting overly aggressive; she may just be trying to let you know she likes you. Be polite and kind, and say something like, "You seem like a nice girl, but I just need to let you know that I'm not interested right now in a relationship." If she persists, recruit some friends to sit around you at lunch so that there's not a place for her to sit down next to you.

Situation #6: You are at a party or a gathering with friends, and a girl becomes physically aggressive.

Suggestion: Immediately tell the girl you are not interested, and then leave the party. If necessary, call your parents.

Two Final Exhortations

I know from experience that it is easy to feel overwhelmed as a parent. Nothing in my life compares to the challenges and leadership it took to raise six teenagers to adulthood. But they all made it, and Barbara and I survived it!

The moral and sexual issues discussed in this book are some of life's thorniest and most demanding that we face. It is not just about protecting your son from aggressive girls; it's also about preserving his innocence and teaching him how to live in purity and how to walk in obedience to a God who wants the best for him.

Let me leave you with two thoughts:

Do not grow weary of doing good (see Galatians 6:9). Parenting requires vigilance—month after month, day after day, hour after hour. When dealing with issues such as sexual purity and aggressive girls, it can feel like an endless battle. You are fighting against the tide of a culture that wants to pull your son in different directions. Often you're fighting against the attitudes and pride of your son, who wants to establish his independence and may not want to listen to much of what you are saying.

Sometimes the battle is your inability to communicate in a way that he can hear.

Don't give up, no matter what. Stay involved in your son's life. Keep on discussing these issues, even when it feels uncomfortable, and even when it feels like you're not having an impact. Remember that parenting is not a sprint but a marathon. One of my favorite quotes by C. H. Spurgeon is appropriate at this point: "It was by perseverance that the snail reached the ark."

Trust God with your son. Pray for and with your son, and fix your eyes on Christ. You can follow all the advice I give you in this book and faithfully work through the seven conversations I suggest, but in the end you cannot control how your son will make his choices. What a comfort it is, then, to know that God is in control and that He has a plan for your son. Your confidence in parenting should be based not only on your knowledge and ability, but on God.

Once you realize that your son's life is in God's hands, you will be motivated to pray continually. Every day your mind is filled with dreams, concerns, and desires for your son. Bring all those before God. Pray for the situations and temptations you know he will face. Pray that God would lead him to friends who will be a positive influence. Pray that he will develop a passionate relationship with God, learn to trust Him with his decisions, and confess his mistakes to God quickly.

Joshua 1:9 tells us, "Be strong and courageous. Do not be frightened, and do not be dismayed, for the Lord your God is with you wherever you go." My prayer is that these words will be true of you as you press into your son's life and train one of the next generation's leaders.

7 Questions You Should Ask Your Daughter

The questions that follow are a starting point to engage your daughter in meaningful conversations about how girls are becoming increasingly aggressive in relating to young men. It is clear that the fifth and sixth grades are pivotal times to begin having conversations around these issues. While you'll want to be sensitive to your daughter's maturity level and readiness to discuss these things, you'll also want to be ahead of the wave, preparing her for a life that includes changing relationships with guys.

It's important to note that these questions are designed to initiate multiple conversations and discussions with your daughter throughout middle school and high school. These questions should not be viewed as a "one time" opportunity to address these issues. You'll need to listen, observe, and encourage her all the way to adulthood.

The questions are listed in a recommended order, but by listening to and being intentionally involved in your child's circumstances at school and social interactions between boys and girls, you may decide to ask some of the more difficult questions earlier.

1. What do you think it means to be an "aggressive" girl? What problems do you see with this kind of behavior?

   Use this discussion to help your daughter understand what the term "aggressive" means when used to describe girls who are inappropriately going after boys.

2. As you watch your friends and peers, do you see any girls who are going after guys? If so, what are you seeing girls do and how are guys responding? What do you think about it? Do you ever feel tempted to act this way toward guys?

   Talk to your daughter about what she sees happening around her in terms of how guys and girls relate to one another. Areas you will want to discuss include school, parties, youth-group activities, texting, social networking, and television shows and movies.

3. Describe the different groups of girls at your school or youth group. How do the girls in each group relate to guys? Which group do you most identify with? Why?

   Use this opportunity, if necessary, to give honest feedback to your daughter about her choice of friends. Help her to understand the power of influence and how our friends' lives affect us. Read 1 Corinthians 15:33 and discuss this biblical warning about the power of peer pressure.

4. If you had a teenage (or preteen) brother who was being sexually pursued by a girl, how would you feel about that? What would you do?

Sometimes it helps to make a point by appealing to a person's emotions. By putting this discussion in the context of her immediate family, your daughter may better understand—and *feel*—the weight of the issue of aggressive girls.

5. What do you think the differences are between being a guy's friend and being his girlfriend?

Use this discussion to start talking to your daughter about the responsibilities of dating. Let her know that you are in her corner.

6. Does the way a young woman dresses send any type of signal to the young men she interacts with? What are some of the signals she might send? What kind of signals do you want to send to boys by the way you dress?

Use this as an opportunity to help your daughter understand that as her body develops, her clothing choices become a statement about who she is and what she stands for.

7. What do you want in a boyfriend and someday in a husband? Make a list and let's talk about it, not just now but also throughout the years ahead.

Talk with your daughter about exhibiting godly character traits and seeking—prayerfully and patiently—the same kind of traits in a young man.

Notes

Chapter 2

1. Alex Kuczynski, "She's Got to be a Macho Girl," *New York Times*, Nov. 3, 2002, http://www.nytimes.com/.

Chapter 6

1. "Marriage," The 2011 Values and Beliefs poll, Gallup, Inc., accessed March 15, 2012, http://www.gallup.com/poll/117328/Marriage.aspx.

2. "The DCR Report," The National Campaign to Prevent Teen and Unplanned Pregnancy, section J-2, accessed March 15, 2012, http://www.thenationalcampaign.org/resources/dcr/.

3. "Teen Survival in a Sex Crazed Culture," Parenting Today's Teens with Mark Gregston, accessed March 15, 2012, http://www.heartlightministries.org/blogs/markgregston/2011/07/29/teen-sexual-promiscuity.

Chapter 9

1. Amanda Lenhart, "Is the Age at Which Kids Get Cell Phones Getting Younger?" Pew Internet and American Life Project, Dec. 1, 2010, http://www.pewinternet.org/Commentary/2010/December/Is-the-age-at-which-kids-get-cell-phones-getting-younger.aspx.

2. Dennis and Barbara Rainey, *Parenting Today's Adolescent*, (Nashville: Thomas Nelson, 2002), 55.

Recommended Resources

Bishop, Jennie. *The Princess and the Kiss: A Story of God's Gift of Purity* (with audio CD). Anderson, IN: Warner Press, 2009.

Courtney, Vicki. *Five Conversations You Must Have with Your Daughter*. Nashville: B & H, 2008.

—. *Your Girl: Raising a Godly Daughter in an Ungodly World*. Nashville: B & H, 2004.

DiMarco, Hayley. *Not-So-Stupid Parents: Why Your Kids Think You're Weird and How to Prove Otherwise*. Grand Rapids: Revell, 2007.

—. *Sexy Girls: How Hot Is Too Hot?* Grand Rapids: Revell, 2006.

—. *Technical Virgin: How Far Is Too Far?* Grand Rapids: Revell, 2006.

DiMarco, Hayley, and Michael DiMarco. *Cupidity: 50 Stupid Things People Do for Love and How to Avoid Them*. Carol Stream, IL: Tyndale, 2010.

Gresh, Dannah. *8 Great Dates for Moms and Daughters: How to Talk About True Beauty, Cool Fashion, and . . . Modesty!* Irvine, CA: Harvest House, 2010.

—. *Six Ways to Keep the "Little" in Your Girl: Guiding Your Daughter from Her Tweens to Her Teens.* Irvine, CA: Harvest House, 2010.

—. *Six Ways to Keep the "Good" in Your Boy: Guiding Your Son from His Tweens to His Teens.* Irvine, CA: Harvest House, 2012.

Hunter, Dr. Brenda, and Kristen Blair. *From Santa to Sexting.* Abilene, TX: Leafwood, 2012.

Kassian, Mary A. *Girls Gone Wise in a World Gone Wild.* Chicago: Moody, 2010.

an **essential**
man-to-man
conversation

interviewing your
daughter's date

30 MINUTES MAN-TO-MAN

dennis rainey

As a dad, you want to protect your daughter—especially from boys with super-charged hormones. But the thought of talking to these young men can make any man break into a cold sweat. Or reach for a baseball bat.

There is an alternative, though: a one-on-one conversation with every young man who'd like to take her out.

This is more than an interview, it's an opportunity; a chance to set the bar high, to hold your daughter's date accountable for something precious. It's even a chance to build into a young man, communicating to him—and your daughter—the value of a God-honoring relationship.

Get away with
your pre-teen for an
adventure of a lifetime!

Passport2Purity® will guide you and your pre-teen through biblical principles regarding peer pressure, dating and sex. Dennis and Barbara Rainey will lead you through this one-on-one retreat with your son or daughter. It's a great time full of discovery, communication and fun.

PASSPORT2PURITY®

1-800-FL-TODAY • FamilyLife.com